The Suprem

CW01523330

UK SINGLES DISCOGRAPHY

Each Release
Tells a Story

First published in Great Britain in 2025
Copyright © Felix Mensah 2025
Published by Victor Publishing - victorpublishing.co.uk
Felix Mensah has asserted his right under the Copyright, Designs
and Patents Act 1988 to be identified as the author of this work.

All rights reserved. No part of this publication may be reproduced,
distributed, or transmitted in any form or by any means, including
photocopying, recording, or other electronic or mechanical methods, without the prior
written permission of the author.

ISBN: 9798280172272

www.victorpublishing.co.uk

INTRODUCTION

The original members of The Supremes - Florence Ballard, Mary Wilson, Diana Ross, and Betty McGlown - all hailed from the Brewster-Douglass public housing project in Detroit. Originating as the Primettes, they were affiliated with the Primes, whose members, Paul Williams and Eddie Kendricks, subsequently formed the Temptations. Following Ms. McGlown's departure in 1960, Ms. Barbara Martin assumed her position; subsequently, in 1961, the group finally secured a contract with Motown Records, rebranding themselves as the Supremes. Following Martin's exit from the group in early 1962, the remaining members, Ross, Ballard, and Wilson, continued as a trio.

The Supremes' mainstream breakthrough occurred in the mid-1960s, with Diana Ross as lead vocalist and Holland–Dozier–Holland providing songwriting and production. The year 1967 witnessed a renaming of the group Diana Ross & the Supremes by Motown president Berry Gordy; concurrently, Ballard was replaced by Cindy Birdsong. The year 1970 marked Ross's departure to embark on a solo career. Jean Terrell subsequently became a member, and the ensemble's name was reinstated as the Supremes. As the 1970s progressed at pace, the group's rotation of membership continued to evolve, with the additions of Lynda Laurence, Scherrie Payne, and Susaye Greene, before the group's official dissolution in 1977, eighteen years after its inception. Their achievements have solidified their position as one of history's most prominent R&B groups and undoubtedly the first ever superstar 'girl group'.

The meteoric rise of the popularity of The Supremes, undoubtedly facilitated the rise of other African-American recording artists to achieve mainstream superstardom with twelve singles that reached number one on the American Billboard Hot 100. The Supremes, a highly successful Motown group, generated a string of hits. Lead singer Diana Ross established herself as a solo superstar to legendary levels. Florence Ballard died aged 32 of a heart attack on February 22, 1976, while Mary Wilson passed away on February 8, 2021. She was 76.

The Supremes were the highest-grossing Motown act, a status they retain as America's most commercially successful female vocal trio.

The Supremes UK Singles Discography: Each Release Tells a Story examines the British single releases of the renowned and iconic American R&B all-female trio, The Supremes, encompassing both successful and less-remembered singles.

Settle in and delve into the rich history surrounding one of Motown's most celebrated acts from its peak years. The stories behind *Baby Love, Come See About Me, I Hear a Symphony, You Can't Hurry Love, Reflections, Stoned Love, Nathan Jones* and numerous other iconic songs are explored.

As expected, to achieve the tremendous task of putting this project together I had to sit down and sift through numerous magazine & paper clippings, reference books and websites to see this project throughout the planning stages and I hope in it's completed stage that I have achieved it's intended goal and that was to make it both topical and enjoyable.

If it wasn't for the following publications and sites this project would never have came to be:
Joel Whitburn/Record Research/Billboard publications: Top R&B Singles 1942-1999, Billboard Book Of Top 40 Hits, Top Adult Contemporary 1961-1993, Billboard's Hot Dance/Disco 1974-2003. Also Billboard Book Of Number One Albums by Craig Rosen & published by Billboard, Billboard Book of Number One Hits by Fred Bronson & published by Billboard, The Guinness Book Of British Hit Singles & Albums, The Virgin Book of British Hit Singles-Complete UK Chart Data from 1952-2010, NME, Record Mirror, Blues & Soul, Echoes, All Music Guide, Record Collector, Wikipedia, Encyclopedia Of Popular Music, The Official UK Charts Company , Find-A-Grave & Everyhit.com.

I'd personally like to thank the following people who inspired & influenced me to pursue this project and made the hardwork and research all that more worthwhile but importantly very very very special:
Sharon'Motown Tracking' Davis, Dave McAleer, Ralph Tee, Brian J Webster of Rutland Records, Rachael Ryan, all those that I encountered at Radio Nene Valley (to numerous to mention), Lindsay Wesker, Duncan Payne, Eugene 'Josh Joel' Williams Jr, Willie Morgan, Paul Gray of MKFM, James Murphy, Mark Harrington of the 'Motown Café' celebration group, Craig Sullivan, Ricky 'Rumour Castro' John, Shaun EB, Steven Edlin, Emma-Claire Young, Aden Southall, Nigel 'Lloyd' Bevan, Neil 'Funkenstein' Marsh, Matt 'Mattyboy' Facer , Juder Browne, Joel Whitburn, David Nathan, Paddy Grady of PGI Ents, Frank Elson, Mark Devlin, Juls Doherty, D.A aka Deren Ali, Lev-G, Eric Izzle, Justin III Sublyminal English, Jay Quinn, Sheraz Yousaf, David 'DRV' Veale, Adam 'Venom Adda'Williams, Aaron Poole, John Portelli aka DJ John John, Steven 'Car Wash' Altman, Mark 'Beamy' Jeffries, , Timmy of Booom TV, Martin aka DJQ, Karl, Gaz, Graham & co of BTTOS nights, Ash Ben, Poundsy, Steve Brookstein, Kenny Thomas, Vix Perks, Adam Jang/Yeti, SoulMo Funk, Tony 'Soul Explosion Hull' Stephenson, Joelle Valente, Andy Salter, Jaxx McKenzie, Steve Mullen, all those at Yum Yums & Buzz nites, Riq , Barry & Jeremy of RAGE Entertainment, Maison Quatro, Stuart Wilkie , all those at SOUL 4U & 'Bob' & Vijay of M2F.

Big thanks to Paul Preece - officially my longest surviving school friend.

Big thanks also to all those other artists, DJs and record buyers that made this project possibility into a serious reality.

And all you other 'cats' that I have not mentioned in name (you know who you are!) and family who are still making sure that everything is kept real and grounded, Radio Nene Valley for that first positive knock on the door and all the folks at the Northamptonshire County Council Central Library for stopping me becoming part of your furniture!!

My deepest appreciation goes to Merv Payne of Victor Publishing for his patience and understanding as I navigated insurmountable obstacles to bring this project to fruition.

Also remembering the music-loving friends who were tragically taken so prematurely: Richard I. Parker, Criss Brand, Ralph "Ral Ral" Burg, and Michael "Recycled Teenager" Smith.

This book is dedicated to the memories of:
PKA Mensah (1931-2017)
and EM Mensah (1939-2022)

Fe' Mensah 2025

"My love of music by The Supremes dates back to 1964. I was in hospital for around 18 months strapped to a bed frame. My mum and Dad managed to get the hospital to allow me a record player at the side of my bed, so when my family visited me they would bring me new records to play …. one of those was "Baby Love" and I was hooked. I have collected records by The Supremes ever since. I was not lucky enough to have seen the originally line up with Diana Ross in the group, but did see The Supremes in 1973 with Jean Terrell at the ABC Northampton with Arthur Conley as support artist.

Over the years I have saw Diana Ross in concert many times at places like Wembley Arena, NEC Birmingham and my favourite Diana Ross concert at the De Montfort Hall Leicester just around the time the movie 'Mahogany' was being released. The Supremes music will last forever"

Patrick 'Paddy' Grady

Broadcaster and DJ

I have been a fan of the Supremes since 1964, when I heard 'Where did our love go' and first saw them on the first Motown tour of the UK in 1965. I was nearly 15 at the time. Great memories and they have been the soundtrack of my life. Motown music and in particular The Supremes has seen me through lost love, finding true love, marriage and having children. Sixty years later I am still singing and dancing around the kitchen to my favourite tunes. Thank you Berry Gordy and all the Motown acts."

Roger McKenna (Fan)

ABOUT THE AUTHOR

Fe' Mensah was born in South London but raised in the East Midlands, he was a regular contributer to the online R&B magazine 'Blacksheep' and in the past was a regular contributor to the alternative DIY arts fanzine 'Fatdog'. Writing assignments and music are his passionate hobbies.

CONTENTS

The Supremes UK Singles Discography

Love Child b/w Will This Be The Day (Tamla Motown TMG 677)*

I'm Gonna Make You Love Me b/w A Place In The Sun (Tamla Motown TMG 685)*

I'm Livin' In Shame b/w I'm So Glad I Got Somebody (Like You Around) (Tamla Motown TMG 695)*

No Matter What Sign You Are b/w The Young Folks (Tamla Motown TMG 704)

I Second That Emotion b/w The Way You Do The Things You Do (Tamla Motown TMG 709)

Someday We'll Be Together b/w He's My Sunny Boy (Tamla Motown TMG 721)*

Why (Must We Fall In Love) b/w Uptight (Everything's Alright) (Tamla Motown TMG 730)

Up The Ladder To The Roof b/w Bill, When Are You Coming Back (Tamla Motown TMG 735)

Everybody's Got The Right To Love b/w But I Love You More (Tamla Motown TMG 747)*

Stoned Love b/w Shine On Me (Tamla Motown TMG 760)*

River Deep Mountain High b/w It's Got To Be A Miracle (Tamla Motown TMG 777)*

Nathan Jones b/w Happy (Is A Bumpy Road) (Tamla Motown TMG 782)*

You Gotta Have Love In Your Heart b/w I'm Glad About It (Tamla Motown TMG 793)*

Floy Joy b/w This Is The Story (Tamla Motown TMG 804)*

Without The One You Love b/w Let's Make Love Now (Tamla Motown TMG 815)*

Automatically Sunshine b/w Precious Little Things (Tamla Motown TMG 821)*

Your Wonderful Sweet, Sweet Love b/w Love It Came To Me This Time (Tamla Motown TMG 835)*

Reach Out And Touch (Somebody's Hand) b/w Where Would I Be Without You Baby (Tamla Motown TMG 836)*

Bad Weather b/w It's So Hard For Me To Say Goodbye (Tamla Motown TMG 847)*

Tossin' And Turnin' b/w Oh Be My Love (Tamla Motown TMG 859)*

I Guess I'll Miss The Man b/w Over And Over (Tamla Motown TMG 884)*

He's My Man b/w Give Out, But Don't Give Up (Tamla Motown TMG 950)*

Early Morning Love b/w Where Is It i Belong (Tamla Motown TMG 1012)*

I'm Gonna Let My Heart Do The Walking b/w Colour My World Blue (Tamla Motown TMG 1029)*

Love I Never Knew You Could Feel So Good b/w This Is Why I Believe In You (Tamla Motown TMG 1064)

Supremes Medley (Parts 1 &2) (Tamla Motown TMG 1180)*

The Composer b/w Take Me Where You Go (Tamla Motown TMG 999)*

Hit And Miss (Mixes) (Motorcity Records 12 MOTC 88)

Back By Popular Demand (DJ Edit & Original Versions) (Beatin Rhythm BRS 1001)*

Your Heart Belongs To Me b/w Interview with Brian Matthew (Outta Sight RSV 053)

FOREWORD

My affiliation with The Supremes first began in 1965 when I heard those dulcet tones of three black girls from Detroit singing "When The Lovelight Starts Shining Through His Eyes".

The Supremes fan club of Great Britain came into being with the dissolution early in 1966 of the late Dave Godin's 'Tamla Motown Appreciation Society', the superlative fan organisation which up until that time had catered to British fans of all their acts. Having been a member myself, the opportunity to apply for the position of secretary to The Supremes fan club came up, and for me the rest is history.

I ran the fan club for four years and during that time arranged fan club receptions for members whenever the ladies were in town.

For me, I first saw The Supremes live in concert at London's Finsbury Park Astoria as part of 'The Motortown Revue' in 1965 alongside Little Stevie Wonder, The Miracles, Martha & The Vandellas accompanied by The Earl Van Duke sextet.

The Supremes success grew and grew and they produced twelve number one singles on the American Billboard Hot 100, The Motown sound we all loved was combined elements of R&B, Blues, Gospel, Swing and Pop consisting of an instantly recognisable sound of thumping back-beats, strings, horns, guitar, tambourines and handclaps.

My love for The Supremes music (including all line ups) has lasted six decades and will undoubtedly be around for a lot longer than we all will, for sure!

Jim Saphin

www.jimsaphin.com

When The Lovelight Starts Shining Through His Eyes b/w Standing At The Crossroads

(Stateside SS 257) - UK Release Date : Jan 1964

The first official British release for the trio named The Supremes as Motown secured a new British deal with EMI Records with releases initially put out on the Stateside subsidiary logo.

"When The Lovelight Starts Shining Through His Eyes" had all the commercial uplifting hooks befitting the Motown sound and the Holland/Dozier/Holland songwriting team but with barely any sizeable promotion that could benefit a reasonable chart position at least, the song failed to replicate its American Top 30 placing, it didnt even register in the British chart.

However it placed itself into the Australian Top 30 in early 1964.

Its subsequent popularity with British audiences followed a cover version by Dusty Springfield, a leading Motown champion and celebrated icon of the sixties.

"When The Lovelight Starts Shining Through His Eyes" subsequently received recorded cover versions by The Zombies, a prominent Brit Invasion group; The Boones (also on Motown), a sibling vocal ensemble daughters of 1950s/early '60s star Pat Boone and, finally, the now-disbanded electro group, The Brite Futures.

The flip side was the downtempo R&B sound of a minor US hit "Standing At The Crossroads".

The next UK release certainly sent things heading into the right direction.

Whether or not coincidental, this single initiated The Supremes collaboration with Motown's leading songwriters and producers, Holland-Dozier-Holland. This recording may also be classified as their breakthrough achievement, substantially outperforming their prior single releases.

Where Did Our Love Go b/w He Means The World To Me

(Stateside SS327) - UK Release Date: Aug 1964

"Where Did Our Love Go" became the first of five consecutive Supremes songs to make number one on the American Billboard Hot 100 Singles Chart within a year's period - the others "Baby Love", "Come See About Me", "Stop! In the Name of Love", and "Back in My Arms Again" were to follow.

Written and produced by Motown's premier songwriting and production team of Holland–Dozier–Holland, the percolating and pacey beats of "Where Did Our Love Go" topped the American Billboard Hot 100 Singles for two weeks during the August of 1964.

Brian Holland, one third of the songwriting/production trio was adamant that "Where Did Our Love Go" was written with the Supremes in mind as by this time the hits were not as forthcoming as hoped.

While Florence Ballard reportedly desired a more robust single akin to those released by labelmates The Marvelettes and Martha Reeves and the Vandellas, the group harbored reservations about the perceived immaturity of the song; however, recognising its potential commercial appeal and feeling compelled to record the material presented to them, they proceeded.

However, after the producers adjusted the song to Mary Wilson's vocal range, Diana Ross ultimately sang lead - a company playback session convinced Berry Gordy that the song and performance were potential chart-toppers.

"Where Did Our Love Go" indeed was the global juggernaut that provided the three ladies from Detroit that international breakthrough as the single itself went on to reach number one across the border in Canada and across the waters in New Zealand plus it hit the top ten across several European territories including number three in both Britain and Ireland and managed top twenty peaks in both Australia and in Germany.

"Where Did Our Love Go," a Supremes classic, has enjoyed enduring popularity, with diverse artists like The Manhattan Transfer, Soft Cell, Sinitta, and Donnie Elbert all recording their own versions.

A British Motown/EMI reissue program celebrating the tenth anniversary of the Supremes' hits saw "Where Did Our Love Go" re-released after the success of the top twenty re-released hit "Baby Love," but it failed to match that chart performance.

"He Means the World to Me" was the B-side on the UK release.

Baby Love b/w Ask Any Girl

(Stateside SS 350) - UK Release Date : Oct 1964

The Supremes were ready and primed for global domination. Berry Gordy hoping to keep the promising momentum flowing for a follow-up chart-topper for his latest protege's, turned to the Motown-in house songwriting/ production team Holland–Dozier–Holland to create a near-commercial sounding clone of their breakthrough global sensation "Where Did Our Love Go".

The song "Baby Love" aimed to showcase sweet backup vocals and signature ad-libs to establish the Supremes' characteristic sound.

Riding the wave of "Baby Love"'s global success, Motown released the song internationally in autumn 1964, scoring another US number one hit. It reigned supreme on the Hot 100 for a month, and also conquered the Cashbox pop and R&B charts.

The International response was encouraging too, it topped the chart in New Zealand, made number two in the Irish Republic, making the top ten in both Holland & Norway and spending a total of fifteen weeks in the UK top fifty with two of those weeks at number one with the Supremes appearing on Britain's flagship chart show 'Top of the Pops' and were also the first all female group to achieve a British number one, cementing Motown's presence in Britain.... or did it?

It proved a classification nightmare, their biggest hit (peak-wise) was the first ever British number one from the American Motown brand of releases yet issued on the EMI subsidiary logo Stateside in the UK. To legitimise a British Motown achieving the same feat (in which years would show it will happen) Motown with distribution from EMI set up their international "Tamla-Motown" brand specifically for all Motown releases outside the USA.

As for "Baby Love" the British ever-growing love and fascination with the American Motown brand was way too irresistible to ignore as within a decade of it reaching the top spot, it re-entered both the Irish & UK charts all over again this time peaking in the top twenty in both territories.

"Baby Love" was nominated but lost out to Nancy Wilson's "How Glad I Am" for the Grammy Award for Best Rhythm & Blues (R&B) Recording of 1964.

The single's flip side was the melodic mid-tempo "Ask Any Girl" which had the commercial bounce to be beyond the status of flip side or LP track.

19

Come See About Me b/w Always In My Heart

(Stateside SS 376) - UK Release Date: Jan 1965

The Supremes were not the first to release a version of the song that provided them with their third straight number one on US Billboard Hot 100 for two seperate fortnightly runs during December 1964/January 1965.

Nella Dodds, a Wand/Scepter artist, released her recording in late 1964, reaching the Billboard Hot 100's Top 80. However, Motown's quick release of the Supremes' version effectively ended the chances of Dodds' song becoming a bigger hit.

In addition, a German rendition of the song was recorded, its title being "Johnny und Joe".

The song's success extended beyond Billboard; it mirrored its chart positions on Cash Box, topped the Canadian charts, performed strongly internationally (reaching number two in New Zealand and number one in Singapore), and achieved a respectable top thirty placing in the UK. It's also one of their most covered songs; Welsh rock and roll revivalist Shakin' Stevens even charted a version in the British top thirty in Autumn 1987, and fellow Detroiter and blue-eyed soul singer Mitch Ryder recorded it for an album.

A sweeping ballad, "Always In My Heart," comprised the B-side.

Stop! In The Name Of Love
b/w I'm In Love Again

(Tamla Motown TMG 501) - UK Release Date: Mar 1965

Officially the first ever single released on the international Tamla Motown subsidiary of Motown Records - which was set up in the UK in conjuction with EMI Records specifically for American Motown releases - The Supremes' choreography for this song involved one hand on the hip and the other outstretched in a "stop" gesture.

After captivating 1964, 1965 saw the glamorous trio of young ladies participating in the now legendary Motown Revue package touring Britain for the first time to help give the Tamla Motown branch a serious UK launch, with shows up and down the country and with The Supremes being quickly identified as the breakout stars of the label were allocated star and

"Stop! In The Name Of Love" provided yet another American number one single and also a return to the top ten in the United Kingdom, to capitalise on their momentum as rising superstars, they were chosen to appear on a one-off British special The Sound of Motown alongside other Motown-signed acts like Martha Reeves & The Vandellas, Stevie Wonder & The Temptations plus it was hosted by fellow Sixties icon and confessed Motown fan Dusty Springfield and was a spin-off from the popular mid-1960s era show Ready Steady Go.

In contrast to their commercially-driven A-sides, the Supremes' B-side, "I'm In Love Again," offered a more melodic and soulful sound.

Legendary songwriter Burt Bacharach once relayed to Motown founder Berry Gordy that "Stop! In The Name of Love" was a personal favourite song of his. Eddie Holland, Lamont Dozier, and Brian Holland composed this song. Dozier claims an alleged infidelity incident sparked this song's inspiration .

Globally the song charted in Australia reaching the top fifty, it made the top three in Canada, in parts of Continental Europe the peaks were patchy - in Belgium it made the top twenty, In Germany, Iceland and in Luxembourg it reached the top ten and it narrowly missed the top twenty in Holland.

R&B chartwise on the American Billboard R&B chart it made number two, on rival American music industry publications Cashbox and Record World it topped their R&B charts.

Back In My Arms Again b/w Whisper You Love Me Boy

(Tamla Motown TMG 516) UK Release Date: May 1965

Another driving beat penned and produced by Holland-Dozier-Holland.

With "Back in My Arms Again," the Supremes achieved an incredible feat: five consecutive chart-topping hits on the Billboard Hot 100, Cashbox, and Record World, a streak that began with "Where Did Our Love Go," "Baby Love," "Come See About Me," and "Stop! In The Name Of Love""

Across the border in Canada the title topped their chart , also this rolling, feelgood number topped Billboard, Cashbox & Record World R&B singles charts.

The title's popularity among audiences abroad resulted in a varied chart performance for the by now in-demand trio - in New Zealand it reached the top twenty and in both Britain and in Germany it peaked inside the top forty.

The song "Back in My Arms Again" proved remarkably enduring, with diverse artists including Genya Raven, Michael Bolton, Nicolette Larson, Fanny, and High Energy recording their own versions in the years that followed.

The B side was "Whisper You Love Me Boy"

Nothing But Heartaches b/w He Holds His Own

(Tamla Motown TMG 527) - UK Release Date : Aug 1965

Written and produced by the Motown in-house songwriting/production trio Holland-Dozier-Holland, "Nothing But Heartaches" for a while signalled a temporary downturn in their commercial fortunes not making the US top spot and narrowly missing the US top ten (number eleven) but across the North American borders it reached the Canadian top five and across the waters it hit the top ten in Iceland and in Singapore too.

The fervent tone and pitch of "Nothing But Heartaches" closely resembled that of Motown labelmates such as The Four Tops and Marvin Gaye, marking a (minor) departure from the established Supremes' girl-group sound.

It gained a British release in the Autumn of 1965 and the trio undertook a promotional appearance on the popular UK TV show 'Top Of The Pops', unlike their previous hits since their successful UK launch the previous autumn, this single failed to enter the UK's top fifty, only reaching the top twenty of the British R&B chart.

This temporary setback didn't slow the Supremes' momentum; they continued their rapid ascent to superstardom, staying busy with performances and recordings, representing the United States, they were chosen to perform at Holland's annual Popular Song Festival in Amsterdam; they also had scheduled appearances in West Germany, as German versions of their hit singles were climbing the charts there.

"He Holds His Own" was the flipside to the single's UK release and was a mid-paced melodic R&B number reminiscent of their very early recorded work.

The homogenous sonic character of Motown recordings from the 1960s was a product of their standardised songwriting and production methods. This formula was applied to The Supremes' next single. The song "Nothing But Heartaches" was catchy and appealing The calculated move, it seemed, had been overextended, thus interrupting their sequence of highly ranked releases, yet, it represented a considerable setback after the phenomenal achievement of their five previous singles.

I Hear A Symphony
b/w Who Could Ever Doubt My Love

(Tamla Motown TMG 543) - UK Release Date: Nov 1965

After "Nothing But Heartaches" failed to both reach the top ten of the US Hot 100 and break into the UK top fifty , resulting in Motown's release plans to cancel the planned follow up release of the track "Mother Dear" instead under the instructions of Motown, Holland-Dozier-Holland wrote a more modernised, melodic, midtempo and more mature structured number titled "I Hear A Symphony" to replace the previous cancelled track which was reminiscent of their earlier releases.

"I Hear a Symphony," washed away fears at the 'Motown Machine' that the Supremes fame was on the wane as it somewhat miraculously rebounded their chart career to become their sixth American Billboard Hot 100 number-one hit for two weeks in the November of 1965 and returned them back into the British top forty when it peaked inside it.

The flipside "Who Could Ever Doubt My Love" was a midtempo track taken from the "Meet The Supremes" album - both tracks were also recorded by The Isley Brothers.

Interestingly, the song "Love Games" by Belle And The Devotions, which apparently drew inspiration from both "I Hear A Symphony" and the Supremes' earlier hit "Baby Love," earned a respectable Top 20 ranking in both England and Ireland after representing the United Kingdom at Eurovision in 1984.

The success of this title globally was mixed - in New Zealand it reached the top five, in Australia it charted within the top fifty, in Holland it reached the top forty and in Canada on the RPM chart it made the top twenty.

It's known R&B crossover positions were on the American publications for Billboard (number two), Cashbox (number two) and number three on Record World.

My World Is Empty Without You b/w Everything Is Good About You

(Tamla Motown TMG 548) – UK Release Date: Feb 1966

The respected rock music historian Andrew Grant Jackson's claim that the (then) latest Rolling Stones single "Paint It Black" bore a strong resemblance to the Supremes recently released track "My World Is Empty Without You" which is debatable for the most part.

The ambiguous rock-type sound of "My World Is Empty Without You" is yet another commercial Holland-Dozier-Holland composition and production performed by (to date) Motown's most successful chart act - The Supremes.

The song's more broader sound resulted in a somewhat 'lowkey' chart performance for an act established at instantly achieving number one singles - it managed to top the Canadian singles chart but in home territory , it could only manage a position of number five on the Billboard Hot 100 and a peak of ten on the Billboard R&B chart, on the rival magazine charts the picture was equally of a 'concern' - Cashbox Pop number five / Cashbox R&B number seven and over at Record World - Pop number four / R&B number twelve.

Its global performance was inconsistent; it charted highly in Singapore, moderately in Australia, and yet failed to enter the British top fifty.

Released as the B-side, "Everything Is Good About You" is a mid-tempo track echoing the style of the previous hit, "I Hear A Symphony".

Love Is Like An Itching In My Heart b/w He's All I Got

(Tamla Motown TMG 560) - UK Release Date: May 1966

At this juncture The Supremes were only second to The Beatles in terms of success on the American singles charts regarding best selling singles artists.

Initially recorded in 1965, the Holland-Dozier-Holland composition and production "Love Is Like An Itching In My Heart" was finally released in mid-1966, heavily reflecting a much stronger soul music influence, without losing too much of their commercial pop sound - the much harder sound of the single possibly/potentially alienated their establishing pop following as it stalled in the lower reaches of the Billboard top ten and didn't even make the British top fifty.

Nevertheless, this upbeat single made the Canadian top five and placed eleventh on the 'Record Mirror's published British R&B chart.

It also achieved top-ten status on the R&B charts of Billboard, Cashbox, and Record World magazine publications.

It apparently was also a partial inspiration for the Fine Young Cannibals hit "Good Thing" from 1989.

The flip side to this single was the similar brash and bold soul track "He's All I Got" which so-easily could have made a potential A-side , as it had the commercial musical ingredients associated with Motown Records and it indeed in later years had a life of it's own, with it's own uptempo, danceable soul sound finding a cult favour on both the British Rare/Northern Soul and the American Beach Music scenes.

33

You Can't Hurry Love
b/w Put Yourself In My Place

(Tamla Motown TMG 575) - UK Release Date : Sep 1966

The Supremes recorded both "You Can't Hurry Love" and "You Keep Me Hanging On" during the same sessions at Hitsville Studio A in the summer of 1966. Motown's Quality Control team unanimously chose the upbeat, singalong song "You Can't Hurry Love" as the Supremes' next single.

And the momentum continued...

"You Can't Hurry Love" taken from the 'The Supremes A Go-Go' parent album. It became the Supremes' seventh American number-one hit,topping the US Hot 100 for two weeks in the September of 1966, and repeating an identikit feat on not only the Billboard R&B counterpart but also on the Cashbox and Record World chart publications for both Mainstream/pop and R&B music.

The overseas performance was equally encouraging - the single topped the Canadian charts and reached the top ten in several territories including in Asia, Australia as well as in Britain reaching the top three and also topping Britain's own trade industry R&B singles chart

The Supremes also released a version sung in Italian: "L'amore verrà" ("Love Will Come"). The flip side was their take on the Holland-Dozier-Holland composition "Put Yourself In My Place" which was also recorded by other Motown signings like The Isley Brothers , Chris Clark and most notably The Elgins.

A nearly identical cover by Phil Collins revived this feel-good tune in 1983, hitting number one and giving it new popularity with a younger audience.

You Keep Me Hanging On b/w Remove This Doubt

(Tamla Motown TMG 585) - UK Release Date : Nov 1966

The uptempo, gospel and rock-flavoured "You Keep Me Hangin' On" was another composition from the pens of by the Holland–Dozier–Holland songwriting and production team.

"You Keep Me Hangin' On" provided another US Billboard chart-topping single for the Supremes and also for the Motown label.

It's global chart performance was rather a mixture - across the border in Canada it reached number two, in the Antipodean territories it peaked inside the Australian top 30 , in New Zealand it reached the top 20 as it did in both Belgium and in the Irish Republic , In Holland it reached the top 30, in Singapore it peaked at number two and in Britain it climbed inside the top ten. Additional success saw this single top the charts of Billboard Magazine's primary rivals -Cashbox & Record World , also a triple US R&B chart-topper too on all three trade magazines. It also reached number one on the Record Mirror compiled British R&B Singles chart and number four on the Blues & Soul Magazine chart.

Re-released in 1977 to align with Motown/EMI's "Supremes - 20 Golden Greats," the "Double A-side" single featuring "Someday We'll Be Together" (TMG 1080) failed to chart, despite the album's major success.

Subsequent to the Supremes' version, numerous other musical acts have recorded their own renditions. Fellow American recording acts like Vanilla Fudge (whose version was released just months later) and soul singer Wilson Pickett recorded their own takes of it with varying degrees of success. However , the British pop princess Kim Wilde practically overnight revitalised her flagging chart profile by recording and releasing the 'definitive alternative version' exactly two decades on from the Supremes original version (UK number two and USA number one)

Interestingly, both the Supremes' and Kim Wilde's versions of "You Keep Me Hangin' On" are among only six songs to top the American Billboard charts for two different artists. A decade after Kim Wilde's version, Reba McEntire, the queen of American country music, released her own rendition, reportedly inspired by the original Supremes' arrangement.

The flip side to this single's release was with the emotional ballad "Remove This Doubt".

Love Is Here And Now You're Gone b/w There's No Stopping Us Now

(Tamla Motown TMG 597) - UK Release Date: Feb 1967

The primary lyricist of the in-house Motown songwriting and production trio Eddie Holland once quoted that "Love is Here And Now You're Gone" as his personal favourite of all the Supremes song.

The recording sessions took place away from the Detroit area, instead in the West Coast of America in Los Angeles, California for the baroque-tinged flow of "Love Is Here and Now You're Gone", which when released provided yet another American number one song on the Billboard Hot 100 and also topping the Billboard R&B chart too. The performance for the single was globally mixed - across the border in Canada it reached number one, across the oceans , in Holland , Australia and Belgium it made the Top 40 and in Britain it reached the top twenty and the top five on the Blues & Soul magazine chart.

Even while their previous smash hit, "You Keep Me Hanging On," was still on the US Hot 100, the hardworking trio performed their next song on the televised "Andy Williams Show."

Years later, both Michael Jackson and Donnie Elbert added their own versions of the track as B-sides to future releases.

The 'B' side for this release was the percolating and upbeat "There's No Stopping Us Now" which had enough commercial bounce to be a 'topside' of it's own.

The Happening b/w All I Know About You

(Tamla Motown TMG 607) - UK Release Date : May 1967

The Supremes next scheduled single release served as the theme tune for the film 'The Happening' released by Columbia Pictures. Whilst the film flopped and became virtually forgotten, the song topped the American Billboard Hot 100 Singles Chart becoming The Supremes' tenth single in the United States alone.

Written and produced by Holland-Dozier-Holland with Frank DeVol (who was the musical arranger for the film) , "The Happening" with it's bouncy soft rock/ vintage easy listening-style arrangement also captivated the international market, the song's performance was highly impressive - it made the Australian top five, number two in Canada, number six in Britain plus top ten peaks in Holland, Malaysia, Ireland & Switzerland as well as reaching the top twenty in New Zealand and Sweden.

It narrowly missed a top ten placing on the Billboard R&B chart (number 12) and likewise on the rival Record World published R&B chart (number 15). On the Record Mirror compiled UK R&B chart reached number two

This song's B-side was the lively and energetic "All I Know About You."

Reflections b/w Going Down For The Third Time

(Tamla Motown TMG 616) - UK Release Date : Aug 1967

"Reflections" was officially the first Supremes recording to be billed as by 'Diana Ross & The Supremes', it also was a sign of musicality moving with the times , the Holland-Dozier-Holland songwriting/production trio for this particular recording embraced and adapted elements of the burgeoning 'flower power' and psychedelia pop culture in it's sound , following the path undertaken by mainly white rock bands of the era such as Jefferson Airplane, The Grateful Dead, Pink Floyd and most notably contemporaries of The Supremes , like the Beach Boys and the Beatles.

It's claimed that this was the first mainstream hit record to utilize the Moog synthesizer.

This was the penultimate hit to feature Florence Ballard on group duties but a promotional performance on the American TV variety show titled 'Hollywood Palace' featured Florence Ballard's replacement Cindy Birdsong as the incoming member of the Supremes in the Autumn of 1967

As by now expected despite the pending changes of time, the single had an impressive chart performance , it provided an American charttopper on singles charts for Billboard, Cashbox & Record World publications , additionally on the R&B equivalent of those charts reached the top 10.

Internationally the song's performance was a somewhat mixed response - it made the Australian top forty, number three in Canada, number five in Britain plus top ten peaks in Holland & Iceland as well as reaching the top twenty in Ireland and top fifty in Belgium.

Peak on Canadian and British industry trade charts for R&B music made number one.

It also peaked inside the top ten of the Blues & Soul magazine published British soul chart

"Going Down for the Third Time" an upbeat piece of commercial Detroit soul served as the flip side to this single's release.

In And Out Of Love b/w I Guess I'll Always Love You

(Tamla Motown TMG 632) - UK Release Date: Nov 1967

"Summer Good, Summer Bad," was the initial title for the forthcoming Supremes single.

Motown's premier production team Holland–Dozier–Holland recorded the track for the now renamed "In and Out of Love" with the in house Funk Brothers session musicians in Detroit during the same allocated recording sessions as "The Happening" and "Reflections," but latterly for reasons unknown totally rerecorded the track over in Los Angeles. Notably It would be Florence Ballard's final session as an official member of The Supremes.

At this stage , behind the scenes things were close to crumbling point with the main CEO of Motown Records Berry Gordy dropping Ballard from the Supremes, who by this time was struggling with the demands of superstardom and extreme fame as well as seeing the dynamic balance somewhat shift in the group she helped to put together, tragically resulting in an emotional decline and descent into depression and alcoholism and in a professional sense missing scheduled recording sessions and live performances.

Cindy Birdsong, formerly of Patti LaBelle and the Bluebells was enlisted as an official replacement for Florence Ballard.

The recording of "In and Out of Love," was somewhat laden with misfortune aside from the pending personnel replacement and the total re-recording of the instrumentation, plus the songwriting/production team of Holland-Dozier-Holland staged a virtual work mutiny which resulted in a self-imposed work slow down and this track being their penultimate collaborative work with The Supremes.

"In and Out of Love," with its country music-style melody, nonetheless scored another top ten hit domestically and a top twenty R&B hit for the trio.

The singalong title also reached the top ten in Canada and in Holland, the top twenty in Britain, the top thirty in Australia.

Additionally it peaked at number two on the Blues & Soul Magazine published British chart for soul music releases.

Their cover of "I Guess I'll Always Love You" later a hit for the Isley Brothers was the B side to this release.

Forever Came Today b/w Time Changes Things

(Tamla Motown TMG 650) - UK Release Date : Apr 1968

"Forever Came Today," was the final hit collaboration between Holland–Dozier–Holland and the (by now re-named) Diana Ross & The Supremes and was the result of a staged work slowdown by the now despondent songwriting/production trio and with no other recordings readily available by the in demand trio , the melodic single recorded sometime in 1967 was released with Motown using their in-house session singers The Andantes to bolster the background session.

Whilst the impressive hit flow was seemingly everlasting , behind the scenes all was not well as Holland-Dozier-Holland were getting sued by Motown Records for a contract breach spurred by their slowdown work rate action thus forcing Motown head Berry Gordy to enlist new songwriters/producers to work with the Supremes as Holland-Dozier-Holland counter-sued Motown over working practices.

When the dust eventually settled the songwriting/production trio went on to sign distribution deals respectively with Capitol Records and with Buddah Records for their own labels, Invictus Records and Hot Wax Records.

"Forever Came Today" performance was a rather mixed response, the melodic title went on to be a Transatlantic top thirty hit , in Canada it reached the top twenty and in Holland reached the top forty. However it seemed to fare better on the American Cashbox & Record World publication charts making the top twenty on both.

The R&B chart performances were quite impressive by comparison - on US Billboard & Cashbox R&B charts as well as on the Blues & Soul Magazine published chart for British soul music releases it reached the top twenty, it reached the top ten on the US Record World R&B chart as it did on the Record Mirror UK R&B chart.

This release's B-side was the waltzing semi-ballad "Time Changes Things" a much earlier pre-fame recording from six years earlier

While The Commodores revisited "Forever Came Today," The Jackson five's energetic remake propelled the song to a new generation in 1975, peaking at a position within the top sixty on the Billboard Hot 100.

Some Things You Never Get Used To b/w You've Been So Wonderful To Me

(Tamla Motown TMG 662) - UK Release Date : Jun 1968

Was the 'honeymoon period' officially over between the charts and the Supremes?

A slight change in personnel and a somewhat enforced change of songwriting and production team for hire seemed to somewhat signal a brief decline in very high chart peaks

A sign of an astonishing fall or possibly a temporary blip?

The next scheduled release "Some Things You Never Get Used To" written and produced by the husband and wife team Ashford & Simpson was an uptempo dance slanted number, for that moment the shocking high peak decline wasn't reversed as this particular single became the lowest-charting Supremes single ever for five years spurring Motown Records head Berry Gordy to organise and to chair an emergency meeting with reputed songwriters and producers in a Detroit hotel in a vain attempt to help turn around the chart career and profile of Diana Ross & The Supremes, following the departure of the Motown in house songwriting and production team Holland-Dozier-Holland.

The upbeat dance track, "Some Things You Never Get Used To," was a top forty hit in Britain and America, with even greater success in Canada where it made the top thirty, and also performed well on the US Cashbox and Record World charts.

The B side was with the uptempo dancer "You've Been So Wonderful to Me".

On the R&B charts the crossover reception was patchy - It only made the top fifty on Billboard, it made the top twenty on Cashbox and the top thirty on Record World

It also made the Record Mirror published UK R&B chart , reaching the top ten.

Frances Nero, a one-time Motown signing , also recorded a rendition of this song years later for Ian Levine's Motorcity label.

Love Child
b/w Will This Be The Day

(Tamla Motown TMG 677) - UK Release Date: Nov 1968

A slight change in sound and image thankfully halted the decline which befelled the profile and chart career of the re-named pioneering female trio Diana Ross & The Supremes in time for their next planned single release.

However, during this career transition, their performance at the Royal Variety Performance at the London Palladium included Diana Ross's impassioned plea for racial tolerance, which received mixed reactions. At that time, Mary Wilson had a two-year affair with Welsh superstar crooner Tom Jones, while Diana Ross' planned departure from the group to launch a solo career was widely publicized. This wouldn't happen immediately, however.

During this period of their somewhat miraculous second wind revival, "Love Child" title track from their latest album Love Child a notably harder edged sound with near pleading/story telling vocals from Diana Ross was penned and produced by a talented collective named as 'The Clan' (R. Dean Taylor, Frank Wilson, Pam Sawyer, Deke Richards and Henry Cosby) - thankfully signalled the positive upturn in fortunes for the trio in regards to both profile and chart career, it became their 11th number one single on the American Hot 100 and it took just three weeks to climb inside the top ten of the Hot 100 before reaching the chart summit.

A collective relief sigh all around as "Love Child" became a positive global chart smash - When it was released as a single in Canada and in New Zealand it also reached number one in both those territories. Reaching the top fifteen in Britain and Ireland, the top five in Australia, the top twenty in the Netherlands and the top ten in both Sweden and Switzerland, the single peaked at number thirty in Japan.

R&B wise the track performed impressively - on the American Billboard R&B chart it stalled at number two, on both Cashbox & Record World publications for R&B music it topped those charts as it did on the Record Mirror compiled UK R&B chart....however on the Blues & Soul Magazine UK chart for soul music releases it only managed a peak of number 17.

No one will ever forget their performance of the song on the Ed Sullivan Show. Instead of their glamorous stage costumes, the trio opted for natural afros and relaxed, casual clothing.

The revamp seemingly for a time worked.

Almighty Records which specialises in Hi-NRG club music and artists released a remixed version of "Love Child" in 2004 (catalogue number PRALMY CD49)

"Will This Be the Day" , a melodic mid-paced number served as the B side to this single's original UK release.

I'm Gonna Make You Love Me b/w A Place In The Sun

(Tamla Motown TMG 685) [with The Temptations] - UK Release Date : Jan 1969

Thankfully, the Supremes' comeback single, "Love Child," a powerful commentary on illegitimacy, propelled them back to the top end of the singles chart. Berry Gordy, unsurprisingly, pulled out all the stops to ensure their continued success.

For the next single release a team up with fellow Motown-signings The Temptations , resulted from sessions recorded with husband and wife songwriting and production duo Ashford & Simpson between May- September 1968 for a team up album project titled "Diana Ross & the Supremes Join the Temptations"

One of the songs recorded in the sessions the Gamble & Huff and Jerry Ross penned "I'm Gonna Make You Love Me" was initially offered to the British blue-eyed soul singer and fellow Sixties icon Dusty Springfield before American expatriate Madeline Bell and the younger sister of Dionne Warwick ,Dee Dee Warwick were given the chance to record their versions.

In conjunction with the album project Diana Ross & the Supremes and the Temptations performed selected songs from the joint album project on a televised special broadcast on American television in time for the festive season of 1968 (this special was pencilled in for an early 1969 broadcast in the UK) - it featured a somewhat magnetic take on "The Impossible Dream". Perhaps sensing that instead a non-performed album track, "I'm Gonna Make You Love Me" was seemingly popular due to the numerous cover versions that was in current circulation, numerous radio stations started playing it resulting in it getting a single release.

Produced by Ashford & Simpson with Frank Wilson, It was transformed into an irresistible duet with the shared vocal duties between Diana Ross and Eddie Kendricks with Temptations founder Otis Williams providing the spoken interlude break ,unique to this particular version of the song.

Deservedly another global smash on their hands as it topped the Cashbox & Record World Magazine charts, it managed a number two peak on the Billboard Hot 100 and across the border in Canada, additionally it reached the top five in Britain, the top ten in Iceland, Ireland and Sweden , it reached the top twenty in the Antipodean territories and it also charted in Belgium and Holland.

R&B chart wise in America on the Billboard R&B chart it peaked at number two on the rival publications of Cashbox & Record World it went all the way to reach number one.In Britain , "I'm Gonna Make You Love Me" peaked at number two on the Record Mirror UK R&B chart and managed a number five peak on the Blues & Soul Magazine published British chart for soul music releases.

The B side was also extracted from the album project team up , a version of the Stevie Wonder track "A Place in the Sun".

I'm Livin In Shame b/w I'm So Glad I Got Somebody (Like You Around)

(Tamla Motown TMG 695) - UK Release Date: Apr 1969

"I'm Livin' in Shame" penned and produced Frank Wilson, Pam Sawyer, R. Dean Taylor, Deke Richards as a sequel to their most recent American number-one hit single, "Love Child" and reputedly inspired by the plot of the Douglas Sirk 1959 film adaptation of the hard hitting 'Imitation of Life'.

Lyrically it followed the similar hard-hitting subject that patterned "Love Child" , though "Love Child" had a much more mature sound , "I'm Livin In Shame" was almost melodically joyous in it's musicality approach despite the tragedy and sadness in the lyrics and indeed title.

Also for sometime in both Britain and in America , Motown was enjoying it's greatest success where weekly the top 50 or even the top ten wasn't without a Motown issued single in the chart.

During the Spring months of 1969 "I'm Livin' in Shame" anchored the American top ten of the Billboard Hot 100 and peaked inside the UK top fifteen. The title also charted in Australia, Canada, Iceland, Holland and Ireland (it's only other mainstream top ten status was also accomplished in the latter two countries)

On the numerous known R&B charts, it also achieved top ten placements - American Billboard R&B (number eight) , American Cashbox R&B (number eight), American Record World R&B (number seven) and on Record Mirror UK R&B (number nine).

As for the Supremes, their captivating and charismatic frontwoman as well as their glorious outfits for that moment were not rapidly fading away as initially feared.

The lilting ballad "I'm So Glad I Got Somebody (Like You Around)" was this single's release B side.

No Matter What Sign You Are
b/w The Young Folks

(Tamla Motown TMG 704) - UK Release Date : Jul 1969

To shift gears to a more upbeat theme, drawing from the late 1960s counterculture movement and the musical "Hair," Henry Cosby and Berry Gordy created a Supremes track heavily inspired by the music of "Hair."

"No Matter What Sign You Are" is a track incorporating a sitar introduction and stylistic musicality features reminiscent of 'acid rock', was initially pencilled in by Motown as a potential official Diana Ross & the Supremes' final single release, though predictably providing yet another hit single , it's discouraging chart peak made Berry Gordy change tack plus Supremes member Mary Wilson who ironically (alongside Cindy Birdsong) did not partake on the studio recording and was reportedly somewhat dismissive about the track - The Blackberries a female session trio (Venetta Fields, Clydie King, and Sherlie Matthews) actually provided the background vocals during the recording session.

"No Matter What Sign You Are" peaked within the Transatlantic top forty as it did in Australia, It managed a top thirty peak in Canada and it's biggest success was in Holland where it peaked at number two.

R&B wise the single did marginally better on the genre magazine charts - Billboard R&B & Record World R&B (number 17), Cashbox R&B (number 20) and Record Mirror UK R&B (number ten) - obviously the rock-influenced/inspired sound didn't put off global R&B formats.

"No Matter What Sign You Are" may have not been the closing single that Berry Gordy envisaged for Diana Ross & the Supremes but has become a cult of his own somewhat.

The B side to this release was with the ballad track "The Young Folks".

I Second That Emotion b/w The Way You Do The Things You Do

(Tamla Motown TMG 709) [with The Temptations]

Two iconic Motown acts cover another iconic Motown act - not unusual maybe but that concept struck again.

Recap back to 1967, Smokey Robinson and fellow Motown songwriter Al Cleveland were shopping in a local Detroit department store. Robinson purchased pearls for his then wife, Claudette. A mispronounced term of phrase used by Cleveland during the purchase inspired Robinson to write the song which at first was a hit for Robinson's group The Miracles (UK top thirty and USA top five) but was also recorded by Diana Ross & the Supremes teaming up with The Temptations and extracted from the album 'Diana Ross & the Supremes Join the Temptations'

Their team up take on "I Second That Emotion" highlighted undoubtedly by the combined voices of Eddie Kendricks together with Diana Ross , though not released in their homeland, the remake restored both acts into the UK top twenty (number eighteen) - additionally it charted within the Icelandic top twenty and reached number two on the Record Mirror UK R&B chart.

Diana Ross And The Supremes & The Temptations combined torchy take on the revival of the latters earlier "The Way You Do The Things You Do" served as the B-side to the British release.

Someday We'll Be Together b/w He's My Sunny Boy

(Tamla Motown TMG 721) - UK Release Date: Nov 1969

A perfect song that summed up the closing of one decade and the opening of another - the musical bridge between two decades representing a quick bygone past and a hopeful yet close future.

"Someday We'll Be Together" somewhat poignant in title, lyrical content as well as in sound.

The poignant ballad, a masterful contemporary soul arrangement characterised the track's production, achieving a sound that remains captivating.

Penned and initially performed eight years earlier, by Johnny Bristol and Jackey Beavers (as Johnny & Jackey) with Harvey Fuqua was extracted from the official final Diana Ross & the Supremes studio album, the 1969 issued 'Cream of the Crop'.

The somewhat emotional track was designated by the powers as a suitable closing career track from undoubtedly an iconic and groundbreaking vocal trio......However Berry Gordy had other ideas!

Gordy already drawing up plans for the solo career phase of Diana Ross, believed that "Someday" in fact would make a great Diana Ross solo debut track as opposed to a group finale track , however Johnny Bristol the original songwriter and performer Johnny was drawing up a totally new version of "Someday We'll Be Together"....but with plans of having Motown's very own jazz/soul sax man Jr Walker recording it instead!.

By sheer coincidence and chance, Berry Gordy chanced upon the Johnny Bristol recorded instrumental backing track with backing vocals already provided by Maxine and Julia Waters.

"Someday We'll Be Together," was written by Johnny Bristol, Jackey Beavers, and Harvey Fuqua back in 1961 with Bristol and Beavers recorded under the moniker of "Johnny & Jackey" for the Tri-Phi label........fast forward eight years with unfortunately only Diana Ross as a Supremes member on primary vocals on the official released re-take version, the back-ups were not that of Mary Wilson and Cindy Birdsong!

With persistence from Gordy concluded that Bristol's own vocals be added alongside Diana Ross's eventual recorded vocal to enhance the track as well as the co-vocal performance, to be allowed on the final recording of the track.

"Someday We'll Be Together" also served as the finale of Diana Ross &

61

the Supremes' Las Vegas farewell concert on January 14, 1970. During this performance, following considerable conjecture regarding Ross's replacement, Jean Terrell was publicly introduced as the new lead singer, alongside remaining members Mary Wilson and Cindy Birdsong. As of this moment, the group "Diana Ross & The Supremes" was officially disbanded.

Fittingly, the single was the final American number-one hit on the Billboard Hot 100 in the 1960s and the last for the Supremes, marking a perfect end for the decade's most successful American group.

This marked the final of twelve number-one singles on the American Billboard Hot 100 achieved by Diana Ross & The Supremes during their highly successful career in the 1960s.

The overall global performance of this single was certainly mixed - in Britain though it reached number one on both the Record Mirror magazine compiled UK R&B chart and on Blues & Soul magazine British chart for soul music releases, it peaked at number 13 on the main British singles chart, however in far apart places like Canada, Iceland, South Africa and in Yugoslavia it achieved a top ten placing.

It also became their first hit to crossover to the Billboard AC/easy listening chart making the top twenty.

"Someday We'll Be Together" also charted in Holland, Australia and also making either number one or number two on American Pop & R&B charts for the Record World and Cashbox magazine publications.

During the dominance of this hit single , personal drama within the Supremes was not too far away but this was one of the most disturbing yet - Cindy Birdsong was a victim of an abduction attempt whilst returning to her Los Angeles residence with partner/future husband Charles Hewlett and Mr. Howard Meek, a friend. The assailant who was later unveiled as a maintenance employee in her apartment complex named Charles Collier compelled Ms. Birdsong to restrain the other two individuals before forcing her, at knifepoint, into her own vehicle. Ms. Birdsong subsequently secured her release by unlocking the car door and exiting the moving vehicle on a main busy road stretch. Subsequently, she was admitted to the hospital for treatment of lacerations, contusions, and stab wounds. The reasons behind Collier's crime remained enigmatic....he was rightfully arrested and charged.

Incidentally a 1977 re-release to coincide with the Motown/EMI released 'Diana Ross & The Supremes-20 Golden Greats' served as the 'Double A' with "You Keep Me Hanging On" (TMG 1080) - despite the success of the album the re-release did not chart.

Smokey Robinson wrote and produced "He's My Sunny Boy," the B-side of "Someday," which Ross, Wilson, and Birdsong recorded for the 1968 album 'Love Child'.

Why (Must We Fall In Love) b/w Uptight (Everything's Alright)

(Tamla Motown TMG 730) [with The Temptations]
UK Release Date : Mar 1970

"Why (Must We Fall in Love)" Lead vocals by Diana Ross and Eddie Kendricks, Motown UK obviously still awaiting fresh product from both the newly solo Diana Ross and the somewhat revamped Supremes extracted this midtempo track from the joint 'Together' album project.

Following the highly successful 'Diana Ross & the Supremes Join the Temptations' album project from 1968 which topped album charts in both North America and in Britain, Motown yet again decided to join the talents of two of the label's biggest acts and as a result 'Together', released in 1969 became the last combined project from both acts and was regrettably peak wise didn't match the success of the first project despite interpretations of songs first performed by Frankie Valli, Sly & the Family Stone, The Band as well as songs by fellow Motown signings like Marvin Gaye, Tammi Terrell and Stevie Wonder - nevertheless the performance on album charts registered within the top thirty in both Britain and in North America

In an effort to capitalize on existing success, Motown/EMI UK designated "Why (Must We Fall in Love)" as a potential single, though the chart peak was disappointing (number 31) perhaps the reason for the disappointing chart peak was the unavailability of both a promotional video or personal / promotional appearance from both acts (the latter for obvious reasons) - Nevertheless, it attained a position within the top ten of the Blues and Soul Magazine's British soul chart.

The chart profiles for either The Supremes or Diana Ross and also The Temptations were however at this moment in time were far from over.

The B-side to this UK-only release was their version of the Stevie Wonder/ Sylvia Moy/Henry Cosby composition "Uptight (Everything's Alright)".

Up The Ladder To The Roof b/w Bill, When Are You Coming Back

(Tamla Motown TMG 735) - UK Release Date: Apr 1970

"Up the Ladder to the Roof" became the first Supremes single since the release of "The Happening" three years earlier to be released under the original name "The Supremes" instead of "Diana Ross & The Supremes".

Also officially the first ever Supremes single to feature new frontwoman Jean Terrell.

This marked a fresh beginning for the Supremes, repositioning them as a 1970s act - Frank "Do I Love You" Wilson, who co-wrote the song with New York-based Italian-American songwriter Vincent DiMirco, also produced "Up the Ladder to the Roof."

"Up the Ladder to the Roof"with it's melodic midtempo pace suitably fixed for Terrell's sweet yet strong voice, returned the Supremes back into the UK top ten and also deservedly found a top ten place in (naturally) their homeland , Canada, Iceland, Holland and peaked inside the Australian top forty too.

Crossover wise , on the Billboard R&B chart it anchored the top five, on the Cashbox R&B chart it reached number six, on the Record World R&B chart it managed a number four position peak and on the Blues & Soul magazine's British soul music chart showed the release reaching its highest peak position of number three during an 18-week run.

Incredibly, this single was only their second crossover hit on the Billboard Adult Contemporary chart, reaching the top thirty.

The trio's new image got off to a great start; their hit single was climbing the charts just as their former/original lead singer debuted her solo track, the anthemic "Reach Out and Touch (Somebody's Hand)," a song penned and produced by Ashford & Simpson shockingly and unexpectedly underperformed (in comparison to "Up the Ladder to the Roof") beyond expectations temporarily placing doubt in the press whether the split was a 'mistake' - for a while, the new Supremes seemed unstoppable, continuing their string of hits from a decade earlier, while Diana Ross, now a solo artist, was yet to achieve the superstardom and legendary status that she was destined for.

The B-side to "Up the Ladder to the Roof" was the uptempo dancer "Bill, When Are You Coming Back".

Everybody's Got The Right To Love b/w But I Love You More

(Tamla Motown TMG 747) - UK Release Date : Jul 1970

Temporarily in terms of pop culture , the tables turned despite a great start for the new look Supremes line-up , despite being produced by Frank Wilson and written by Lou Stallman, the socially conscious follow-up single, "Everybody's Got the Right to Love," only reached the top 30 on the US Billboard Hot 100, but fared better on other charts, reaching the top 20 on Cashbox and Record World, as well as in the Netherlands and Canada - whilst Diana Ross was enroute to score her first ever solo number one single (on the US Hot 100) with a distinct re-telling of the Ashford & Simpson track "Ain't No Mountain High Enough".

Despite its smooth sound, "Everybody's Got the Right to Love" surprisingly failed to chart in Britain, marking their first chart miss in four years; however, it did reach the British soul chart's top ten, as ranked by Blues & Soul magazine - it also managed top ten placings on American R&B charts for both Cashbox and Record World publications whilst over at Billboard R&B it narrowly missed the top ten. It also made the top thirty on Billboard's Adult Contemporary chart.

"But I Love You More" a melodic and smooth soul ballad was the B-side to this release.

Stoned Love b/w Shine On Me

(Tamla Motown TMG 760) - UK Release Date : Jan 1971

"Stoned Love" was (unbelievably) The Supremes final hit to reach the top ten on the American Billboard Hot 100 and also their last single release to top the R&B equivalent too.

Penned by the song's producer Frank Wilson alongside budding Detroit-based teenage songwriter Kenny Thomas whom by sheer chance was discovered by Wilson who was listening to a radio talent show - as a result mutual contact was arranged and a meeting set up in which Thomas played songs he had written on a two-string guitar including an embryonic version of "Stoned Love" which impressed Frank Wilson whom just days later met up again with Thomas at his own home but this time bringing along Supremes member Mary Wilson with him!

Perhaps inspired by Stevie Wonder who at one time recorded an off-genre jazzy MOR album under the reversed spelling alter ego of "Eivets Rednow", the Kenny Thomas writing credit of "Stoned Love" was as seen on the label as the reversed spelt "Yennek Samoht" (reportedly also inspired by Nina Simone) - please not the extra "e"!

As the song started to rise to chart life , unintentional controversy was not that far away as plenty of people assumed by the song title alone that it was a paen to the post-flower power era drug culture but according to songwriter Thomas was lyrically about the definition of the concepts of bonding between each and every one and in fact if in lyrical tone but certainly not in it's style reminiscent of the message-themed material of Sly & The Family Stone.

Also apparently Motown head Berry Gordy didn't care much for the track!

With the rumoured drug association long faded , the soft-rock style of "Stoned Love" highlighted by the sweet soul lead vocal of Jean Terrell, started to make it's chart impact on American home soil hitting the top ten on the American magazine charts for Billboard, Cashbox and Record World publications , hitting number one on the R&B equivalents on all those magazine charts - globally it's chart appeal was a somewhat mixed response , it reached the top ten in Canada, Iceland and also in Singapore, it also charted in Ireland, Belgium and in Australia but reached it's highest international position in Britain at number three - It remains the biggest post-Ross-era Supremes' hit in Britain, also topping the Blues & Soul magazine published British soul music chart. Furthermore, it cracked the Billboard Adult Contemporary top thirty.

The only major hit taken from the studio album "New Ways But Love Stays" which managed a top twenty peak on the BIllboard R&B Album chart.

'Stoned Love' refused to fade as some 18 years later it was re-recorded by the splinter trio Former Ladies Of The Supremes AKA FLOS.

The bubblegum-laced soul/funk groove "Shine On Me" was the B-side to this release.

As the American chart run (and indeed at times the UK chart run) of major hits for the Supremes during this period became somewhat unpredictable and patchy, there's life still left in the Supremes yet.

River Deep Mountain High b/w It's Got To Be A Miracle

(Tamla Motown TMG 777)[with The Four Tops] - UK Release Date: Jun 1971

Motown's hefty confidence in the Supremes as still a marketable, relatable and saleable in the already ever and inter changing early '70s era saw the powers professionally pair them up with another high selling and iconic Motown signed act - The Four Tops - under the rather imaginative sub-moniker 'The Magnificent 7' , their unofficial name but also the name of the album project they recorded.

Inspired by the successful collaborations between the Supremes and the Temptations in the late 1960s, Motown sought to replicate this formula for their leading female group, pairing them this time with the Four Tops, who were also enjoying parallel chart success in both the UK and US.

'The Magnificent 7' reverted to both group names instead of the spin-off The Magnificent 7 team up name - the album however was titled 'The Magnificent 7' and was laden with cover versions of a wide range of material rooted in different genres and extracted was their pulsating version of "River Deep, Mountain High" b/w "It's Got To Be A Miracle (This Thing Called Love)" (for the UK market)

"River Deep – Mountain High" without doubt and danger returned the Supremes name back into the global singles charts, The Supremes & Four Tops combined vocal prowess on this rousing gospel-like take on this Phil Spector, Jeff Barry and Ellie Greenwich composition first recorded just five years earlier by fiery husband and wife team Ike & Tina Turner was produced by Ashford & Simpson and arranged by Paul Riser.

The global chart performance for this revival was indeed encouraging and impressive - on the premier American industry charts it charted within the higher reaches of the top twenty, performed even better on the R&B equivalents reaching the top ten.

The single was a notable international success, charting in the top forty in both Holland and Belgium, and peaking within the top twenty in Britain, Canada, Ireland, and South Africa.

It climbed to its highest-ever position of number two on the British soul music chart in Blues & Soul magazine.

The B-side to the British release was the soul shuffling midtempo swayer "It's Got To Be A Miracle (This Thing Called Love)".

It's worth noting that the UK sales of 'The Magnificent 7' parent album exceeded 30,000 copies sold , leading to a peak chart position of number six on the British album chart.

71

Nathan Jones
b/w Happy (Is A Bumpy Road)
(Tamla Motown TMG 782) - UK Release Date : Aug 1971

"Nathan Jones" the next scheduled British release single for the Supremes was from the pen of ex-Chess Records staffwriter Leonard Caston alongside songwriter Kathy Wakefield and perhaps from a perspective point of view their most experimental track to date i.e the producer of the track Frank Wilson used the progressive rock style as the musical bounce and inspiration for "Nathan Jones" with not only help from the musicality of by The Funk Brothers but also the primary vocals performed simultaneously by all three Supremes members with additional vocals provided by Clydie King, which in turn would be used to dub over to make a 'multi-layered' vocal pattern against a flanger sound board effect.

"Nathan Jones" musically was a stark contrast from the Supremes material from just a few years earlier in which (still in the Ross-fronted era) the songs were either about social conscious themes, traditional themes of love and romance or the dabbling into experimental sounds - "Nathan Jones" was a game changer of sorts as it's unique musical blend of alternative rock and soul characterized the transition of Motown's top-charting all-female group into the early 1970s, moving beyond the flower-power era.

It had quite an impressive chart life in both Britain and America - their last single to chart within the UK top five , whilst it settled for a top twenty position on the Billboard Hot 100 - on both rival publications Cashbox and Record World it reached the top ten on both their sales/singles charts

Crossover wise , it achieved a top ten placing on the Billboard, Cashbox and Record World R&B charts and in Britain on the Blues & Soul magazine chart it reached as high as number three.

The unique alternative rock 'n' soul fusion sounds of "Nathan Jones" proved popular enough to crack the top thirty of Billboard's Adult Contemporary chart, defying expectations in the US easy listening market.

Interestingly, as "Nathan Jones" hit the peak of the British charts, Diana Ross's ballad "I'm Still Waiting" reached the top, marking her first solo number one single in the Britain.

"Nathan Jones" was also the most successful single to be extracted 'Touch' studio album - to date was their 23rd recorded album project. The British female vocal trio Bananarama twice recorded a cover of "Nathan Jones", firstly on their album 'Wow!' and later for their first compilation. 'The Greatest Hits Collection', where it is featured in a revised version. A return to their trademark sound "Happy is a Bumpy Road" was the B-side to this release.

73

You Gotta Have Love In Your Heart b/w I'm Glad About It

(Tamla Motown TMG 793) [with The Four Tops] - UK Release Date: Nov 1971

Lead vocals provided by Jean Terrell and Levi Stubbs, another momemtum maintaining 'Magnificent 7' team up, the singalong ,joyous "You Gotta Have Love in Your Heart" issued as a single at the tail end of 1971, and was taken from the Supremes & Four Tops team up 'The Return of the Magnificent 7' album project.

Both acts appeared on the BBC's flagship show, "Top Of The Pops," to perform and promote the track, boosting its chart performance to the top thirty in Britain and also making number four on the Blues & Soul Magazine chart for soul music releases.

The single had already peaked inside the top sixty on the American Billboard Hot 100, Cashbox and Record World charts , inside the top fifty on the Billboard R&B chart but fared far better on the Cashbox and Record World R&B charts charting respectably within their top thirty.

The gentle ballad "I'm Glad About It" was this single's B-side.

It is noteworthy that 1971 represented the peak of the Supremes' success on the British singles chart in the post-Diana Ross era, with the successful release of "You Gotta Have Love in Your Heart" helping to solidify that claim.

Floy Joy
b/w This Is The Story
(Tamla Motown TMG 804) - UK Release Date: Feb 1972

This recording, produced and written by William "Smokey" Robinson, showcases lead vocals by Mary Wilson and Jean Terrell, with additional vocal support from the Andantes, and instrumental performance by Marv Tamplin and the Funk Brothers. What could possibly go wrong with the Supremes next scheduled release?

Evoking their mid-1960s style, the smoothly flowing and wistfully catchy "Floy Joy" achieved a final top twenty placement for the Supremes on the American Billboard Hot 100, Cashbox, and Record World charts, and represented their penultimate top ten success in the United Kingdom.

R&B chart wise (as expected) the peak outlook was a mass improvement - making the top five on the American Billboard and Record World magazine R&B top five as it did on the Blues & Soul magazine British soul chart and making the American Cashbox Magazine R&B top ten.

Its Billboard Adult Contemporary chart performance culminated in a top forty ranking.

The dramatic ballad "This Is The Story" was the B-side to this release.

Without The One You Love b/w Let's Make Love Now

(Tamla Motown TMG 815) [with the Four Tops]
UK Release Date: May 1972

Tamla Motown released a single in Britain during May 1972; the A-side was "Without the One You Love," and the B-side was "Let's Make Love Now." Both sides taken from the 'Magnificent Seven' album project between the Supremes & the Four Tops.

The Four Tops' original recording of "Without the One You Love (Life's Not Worth While)" preceded their later, known version by eight years. It followed their Motown chart debut, "Baby I Need Your Loving," and while it almost made the Billboard Top 10, its follow-up single underperformed, missing the Top 40. Despite this, it was more successful on the Cashbox R&B chart, reaching the top twenty.

The Supremes and the Four Tops recorded a rousing, upbeat cover of the Four Tops' original song for 'The Magnificent 7' album. The group's lead singers, Jean Terrell and Levi Stubbs, handled lead vocals. A song penned by the Holland-Dozier-Holland songwriting trio, though production duties on this revised version handled by the team of Nickolas Ashford, Valerie Simpson, and Frank Wilson.

Although it didn't chart on the main UK top fifty, it did reach the top forty of the Blues & Soul magazine's British soul chart.

This specific version's popularity extended to Asia, achieving a top twenty ranking in Bangkok.

The single was not released in America.

The B-side was the smooth , melodic and soulful "Let's Make Love Now".

Automatically Sunshine b/w Precious Little Things

(Tamla Motown TMG 821) - UK Release Date: Jun 1972

"Automatically Sunshine," an upbeat mooded, singable summer anthem, reached the top ten in Britain, representing the Supremes' final single to attain this level of chart success and their penultimate American top-forty entry. From this point, the Supremes concentrated more on live work , while subsequent singles, albums and line-up changes failed to recapture their grip as a chart act or even as a casual interest for the record buyer music and trends were rapidly on the move.

Smokey Robinson penned "Automatically Sunshine," the second single extracted from the Supremes' most recent studio album 'Floy Joy'. It featured founding/original Supreme Mary Wilson and replacement lead Jean Terrell sharing joint vocal leads on the song.

"Automatically Sunshine" was the Supremes' second-to-last top forty hit on the American Billboard Hot 100, but their final top-ten single in the UK, reaching number ten. Chart success was greatest in Thailand, where the song reached number three. Further success was seen in Iceland (top ten) and Canada (top forty).

Additionally "Automatically Sunshine" charted on R&B formats on magazine charts- Billboard (number 21), Cashbox (number 31) and Blues and Soul (number two).

"Automatically Sunshine" had a renewed interest during the late 1980s due to it's use in a UK TV advertising campaign for laundry powder.

"Precious Little Things," a piece blending jazz and waltz styles, comprised the B-side of this release.

Your Wonderful Sweet, Sweet Love b/w Love It Came To Me This Time

(Tamla Motown TMG 835) - UK Release Date : Nov 1972

Originally recorded by Kim Weston but shelved for nearly four decades, Smokey Robinson's composition "Your Wonderful, Sweet Sweet Love" was finally released as a single when recorded by the Supremes in 1972, and was the last single to be taken from their album 'Floy Joy'.

Furthermore, this was the final Supremes recording to include Cindy Birdsong, whose temporary departure resulted in Lynda Laurence's brief tenure with the group.

Although "Your Wonderful, Sweet Sweet Love" exhibited an unusual blend of bubblegum, funk, and soul, it failed to attain the level of international chart success enjoyed by previous releases. What could have been a huge global hit, maybe even higher than top forty, was lost as an unpromoted 45.

Despite peaking at number sixty on the Billboard Hot 100, the song achieved a position within the top twenty-five on the American Billboard R&B chart. Furthermore, it claimed the top spot on the British Breakers/Bubbling Under chart (number fifty-one overall) for the week commencing November 18, 1972. Its highest position on the British soul singles chart, as published in Blues & Soul magazine, was within the top fifteen.

It certainly seemed for the now , the charts and the Supremes were becoming more and more estranged as both American and British musical tastes were rapidly changing as the decade progressed, though ironically, the two Supremes singles charting in Britain during 1972 both reached the top ten, outperforming/outpeaking Diana Ross's lone British charting track that year; even so, the somewhat challenging title of "Doobedood'ndoobe, Doobedood'ndoobe, Doobedood'ndoo" reached the British top twenty.

The midtempo dancer "The Wisdom of Time" also helmed by Smokey Robinson served as the B-side to the British release.

Reach Out And Touch (Somebody's Hand) b/w Where Would I Be Without You Baby

(Tamla Motown TMG 836)[with the Four Tops] - UK Release Date: Nov 1972

Did the release of this version aim to counter the downturn in Supremes product sales? Or indeed a somewhat unintentional move to relive a recent past?

In 1970, whilst Diana Ross first post-Supremes solo release "Reach Out and Touch" was making it's chart life as her solo debut, her former group, The Supremes with help from fellow iconic Motown act The Four Tops also recorded it in a cosmic level of irony. The Supremes, by this time consisted of new lead Jean Terrell with Mary Wilson and Cindy Birdsong whom together with the Four Tops, collaborated on a duet for their joint album project, "The Magnificent Seven" released globally by Motown in late 1970.

Precisely two years later, and mere weeks after the disappointing chart performance of "Your Wonderful Sweet, Sweet Love," Motown UK released another track from a two-year-old album; this release possibly served as a final promotional effort, as the Four Tops had not long departed from the Motown Records roster and joined ABC Records instead after much interest from other labels.

Whether or not it w as a commercially driven venture, the song "Reach Out And Touch (Somebody's Hand)" warrants consideration.

The B-side to the British release was "Where Would I Be Without You, Baby".

Bad Weather b/w It's So Hard For Me To Say Goodbye

(Tamla Motown TMG 847) - UK Release Date: Mar 1973

The Supremes' chart success had somewhat dramatically waned by this stage.

Following the recording of the group's 1972 album, 'Floy Joy', Cindy Birdsong departed the Supremes on a maternity leave basis and was temporarily replaced by Lynda Laurence, formerly a background vocalist for Stevie Wonder's back-up act Wonderlove. Although every song included Birdsong, the album cover featured Lynda Laurence's image. With Laurence in the lineup, the recording of "The Supremes Produced and Arranged by Jimmy Webb" was initiated, however commercial success eluded the album in spite of positive reviews.

Despite setbacks, Laurence sourced the aid of Wonder, in the group's pursuit of a fresh contemporary sound . Wonder produced some tracks including the planed forthcoming single "Bad Weather," a break away from the trio's sweet sound sound, replaced with a hard edged approach.

"Bad Weather", a Stevie Wonder co-composition with Ira Tucker Jr., Lynda Laurence's brother; Wonder also produced it.

Preceding its United States release, this record achieved critical acclaim in Great Britain; these positive reviews were then leveraged in its American marketing. The record's failure to reach a respectable chart peak is inexplicable. A single rationale exists. Following Diana Ross's eventual successful solo career launch, Motown's promotional and priority efforts concerning the Supremes were markedly reduced as time progressed.

Issued in both Britain and in America during the March of 1973 , the single signified the last charting release featuring Jean Terrell as the lead vocalist for the Supremes, as well as Lynda Laurence's second and final appearance on a Supremes single.

Notwithstanding encouragement from the trio and Wonder, Motown's promotional efforts for "Bad Weather" proved moderately insufficient. Mary Wilson later recounted that Terrell and Laurence did not value the song in high esteem. With the passages of time, "Bad Weather" attained cult classic status, its significance as a forerunner of the disco era now acknowledged by historians of dance music.

Jean Terrell's departure from the Supremes followed the single's release, Lynda Laurence subsequently left the group following her pregnancy.

The song eventually peaked inside the British top forty (their last new single to do so) and reached the top ninety in America.

R&B crossover wise , it only reached the top eighty on the Billboard R&B chart and did considerably better on the Blues & Soul Magazine published British Soul chart spending ten weeks and peaking inside the top twenty.

Contrary to expectations, their international growth remained relatively robust as "Bad Weather" rapidly gained popularity and reached the top of the charts in Puerto Rico.

Subsequent recordings of "Bad Weather" included a 1978 rendition by American songstress Melissa Manchester on her album 'Don't Cry Out Loud', and a 1994 version by the Dutch singer Mathilde Santing and featured on the 'Under a Blue Roof' album.

Regarding the Supremes...... now was there a decline in Motown's primary focus on its formerly most popular and first true superstar act - even with the trio's continued high level of performance?

The timeline for the next Supremes project indicated a two-year development cycle.

"It's So Hard For Me To Say Goodbye" was the B-side.

Tossin' And Turnin'
b/w Oh Be My Love
(Tamla Motown TMG 859)- UK Release Date: Jun 1973

To keep the Supremes name in the chart , Motown/EMI UK decided to extract a track from the often ignored "The Supremes Produced and Arranged by Jimmy Webb" pre-ceding their recorded work with Stevie Wonder by one year and in a sense were returning to the past in more ways than one. It was also Jean Terrell's final contribution as lead vocalist for The Supremes was on this particular studio album.

The song "Tossin' and Turnin'," a composition by Ritchie Adams and Malou René, enjoyed initial release by Bobby Lewis in 1960, marking a significant R&B/Pop crossover achievement before Motown's rise to prominence - the Supremes upbeat rock and roll-like revival of it was released in the UK

Despite not charting in Britain and only reaching the American Billboard R&B album chart's top thirty, the album "The Supremes Produced and Arranged by Jimmy Webb" reportedly sold over 100,000 copies, contradicting assertions of inadequate commercial performance. Even with Motown's promotional efforts, the album's performance would likely not have significantly improved. The lack of airplay for this album appears to have stemmed from radio programmers' decisions, leaving unclear what measures Motown or indeed the act itself could have taken to increase radio exposure. Mary Wilson's account indicated that some radio DJs were not cognizant of the album's presence in their inventory, underscoring the indifference of the radio programmers. The underperformance of the single "Bad Weather" likely contributed to a worsening of negative perceptions.

The song "Tossin' and Turnin'" had a limited chart history, appearing for only two weeks on the Blues and Soul magazine's British soul chart, reaching a peak position within the top fifty.

The B-side to this release was the Smokey Robinson / William Moore composition "Oh Be My Love".

I Guess I'll Miss The Man b/w Over And Over

(Tamla Motown TMG 884) - UK Release Date: Jan 1974

Was the British enthusiasm for Motown music/artists diminishing?

Concurrently during this era on the British singles chart, recordings by seminal Motown-signed artists such as the Temptations, Marvin Gaye, and of course, the Supremes either failed to maintain momentum or underperformed relative to expectations. Even relatively newer and younger Motown-signed acts like the Jackson Five and their enigmatic lead singer, Michael Jackson, faced similar challenges.

During this period, only Stevie Wonder, a burgeoning superstar, and, paradoxically, Diana Ross, the Supremes' original lead singer, were truly the only Motown-signed acts that were still achieving consistent success of the highest levels on the British singles chart.

Away from commitments and responsibilities with the trio, Wilson married Pedro Ferrer, a Dominican businessman and her selected manager for The Supremes, in a Las Vegas ceremony in May 1974. The couple produced three offsprings: a daughter, Turkessa (born 1975), and two sons, Pedro Antonio Jr. (born 1977) and Rafael (1979–1994). In 1981, Wilson and Ferrer were legally divorced.

Evidently, a futile effort was made to preserve the Supremes' presence on the British charts, Motown UK orchestrated an official release of the Supremes gentle version of "I Guess I'll Miss the Man" penned by Stephen Schwartz and adapted from the stage musical 'Pippin'. Sherlie Matthews and Deke Richards served as producers for the recording.

In 1972, Motown released the single in America; however, it was excluded from the British market at the time , deemed unsuitable. The track was extracted from their album, "The Supremes Produced and Arranged by Jimmy Webb" - Its highest ranking was within the top twenty of Billboard's Adult Contemporary chart; on the Billboard Hot 100, it reached the top ninety.

In Britain, the almost two-year old track unfortunately didn't make that much expected impact.

The B-side was the two year old extracted Smokey Robinson production and composition "Over And Over".

He's My Man b/w Give Out, But Don't Give Up

(Tamla Motown TMG 950) - UK Release Date : Aug 1975

In 1975, the Supremes' personnel underwent further changes, with Mary Wilson remaining, Cindy Birdsong rejoining, and Scherrie Payne becoming a new member.

The innovative trio set their sights on capitalising on the ascendant popularity of disco music.

The lead single from The Supremes' eponymous 1975 comeback album was "He's My Man," signifying their musical comeback.

The single ultimately reached positions of number 69, number 77, number 65, and number 15 on respectively the Billboard, Cashbox, Record World, and British Blues & Soul R&B charts, and achieved the number one spot on Billboard's Disco chart.

Although "He's My Man" achieved the number one position on the recently created American Billboard Disco Chart, its promotion and dissemination were reportedly deficient owing to an apparent calculated effort to phase them out.

To promote "He's My Man," they undertook numerous high-profile television appearances in both the United States and the United Kingdom within the designated timeframe. The song received substantial airplay on UK radio and television, featuring several appearances by the Supremes; however, it did not achieve the anticipated chart performance.

The British bypass was baffling as both the single and the parent album benefited from extensive local promotion and enjoyed widespread availability at record stores. The trio engaged in extensive press interviews and television appearances in Britain alone . Plus the fact that Tony Blackburn selected "He's My Man" for his Radio 1 "Record of the Week" segment, a designation typically guaranteeing chart success, proved to be an exception. Despite this, the song was a welcome and pleasant surprise, showcasing the Supremes' capacity to create high-quality recordings independently of the by now superstar Diana Ross and Berry Gordy's support.

"He's My Man" also represented a missed opportunity. A strategic embrace of the disco trend would have allowed the Supremes to retool as 'disco divas', ironically a feat that former frontwoman Diana Ross later accomplished. Unfortunately, it did not come to fruition for the new look trio itself.

The combination of Mary, Scherrie, and Cindy proved to be exceptional. It is regretable that this incarnation of the trio did not achieve significant mainstream success, which might have prolonged their time together and may have maintained both the record buying public and Motown's interest in them as a viable act.

In the early autumn of 1975, the trio garnered significant media attention with two newsworthy events , firstly due to a near-miss during a promotional tour in the UK. The hotel in which they were staying in at the time was targeted in a terrorist bombing. Secondly an ill-judged promotional tour of South Africa was undertaken by the Supremes in late 1975. Despite the fact that black political figures and community members had pleaded with them to reconsider this decision.

The news items didn't help to return them back into the charts.

"Give Out, But Don't Give Up" a midtempo, melodic number in the 'girl-group' vocal tradition served as the B-side to this release.

Early Morning Love b/w Where Is It I Belong

(Tamla Motown TMG 1012) Release Date: 7 Nov 1975

Mary Wilson provides the lead vocals for "Early Morning Love". The single marked the final release from the Supremes self-titled album of 1975.

The song's performance on the popular American television show "Soul Train" led to its achieving sixth place on the Billboard Disco Singles chart and a top ninety placement within the Blues and Soul Magazine British chart for soul music releases.

Their first studio album in almost three years failed to meet expectations. Although the group promoted the self-titled album diligently, its overall success was, at best, modestly achieved. However, the burgeoning popularity of dance clubs provided a significant advantage to the group. The significant Billboard Dance chart performance of numerous songs from the album demonstrates the Supremes' continued broad audience reach, notwithstanding relatively low sales figures. A more marked continuation of this trend is observable in the trio's next studio album, released the year after.

The album's and indeed offshoot single's poor performance necessitated a reassessment of approach, a necessary step given the album's failure to re-establish a pioneering musical trio.

"Where Is It I Belong" a gentle, melodic ballad served as the B-side to this release.

I'm Gonna Let My Heart Do The Walking b/w Colour My World Blue

(Tamla Motown TMG 1029) - UK Release Date: May 1976

The year 1976 holds a significant place in the history of the Supremes, marked by the hospitalisation of founding member Florence Ballard during the February at Mt. Carmel Mercy Hospital early due complaints to numbness. The following morning she passed away at the age of 32. In the protracted period following the demise of her musical career, Florence Ballard grappled with significant personal hardships, including alcoholism, depression, and poverty. She suffered a fatal coronary thrombosis, resulting in a heart attack that ended her life while she was planning a musical comeback.

Meanwhile the original frontwoman, Diana Ross ushered her fame level into superstardom during this period becoming a highly successful duel entertainer of both singing and acting.

The Supremes (by now comprising of Mary Wilson, Scherrie Payne and ex-Wonderlove alumni Susaye Green) endured a four-year absence from the top 40 charts and frequent changes in membership by 1976. The double loss of Jean Terrell, Lynda Laurence, and Cindy Birdsong over four years created substantial obstacles for Supremes co-founder Mary Wilson in preserving the group's continuity. Management difficulties under Pedro Ferrer's leadership resulted in Cindy Birdsong's departure, necessitating a further search for a band member subsequent to Scherrie Payne's recruitment (sister of renowned vocalist Freda Payne). To reconstitute the trio, Ms. Wilson subsequently recruited Ms. Susaye Greene, a fellow former background vocalist for the Wonderlove group, possessing remarkable vocal talent.

The disco-driven single, "I'm Gonna Let My Heart Do the Walking," a 1976 release, was composed by Eddie and Brian Holland (formerly of Holland–Dozier–Holland). Notably, this single was the first by the Supremes since "Your Heart Belongs to Me" in 1962 to include four distinct members in its lineup: Mary, Scherrie, Cindy (who was leaving the group), and Susaye (who was joining). This song holds significance as the last time the trio achieved a top forty placing on the Billboard Hot 100 in America, preceding their disbandment in 1977.

Despite failing to reach the British top fifty, the title enjoyed a twelve-week run on the Blues and Soul Magazine's British Soul Singles chart, ultimately falling just shy of reaching the top twenty.

It was more of a multi-format crossover hit in their homeland - on the Billboard R&B chart it reached the top thirty, on the Cashbox Top 100 it made the top sixty as it did on the Record World equivalent. On the Cashbox R&B chart it reached the top twenty as it did on the Record World R&B Chart ,but it's greatest success was on the disco music charts for Billboard and Record World.

This single's B-side was "Colour My World Blue," which was also recorded by the Southern soul singer Ann Sexton.

Love I Never Knew You Could Feel So Good b/w This Is Why I Believe In You

(Motown TMG 1064) - UK Release Date: Mar 1977

Did the trio the Supremes informally dissolve upon Diana Ross's departure? Do the post-Diana era recordings merit critical acclaim?

In 1976, The Supremes released their twenty-ninth studio album, 'Mary, Scherrie & Susaye', their final recording for Motown Records. The album project constituted a carefully constructed blend of adult-oriented ballads and disco/dance-oriented material.

"Love, I Never Knew You Could Feel So Good" was the last new recording from the Supremes to be released in Britain , having already made the top five on the Billboard Dance chart, it only registered on the Blues and Soul Magazine published British Soul chart and despite spending fourteen weeks on that specific chart it hovered just above the top fifty mark with no signs of a positive chart rise.

The Supremes' final performance as a group took place on June 12, 1977, approximately three months after the single's British release, at London's Theatre Royal, Drury Lane. The performance featured the final iteration of the Supremes- founding/original member Mary Wilson alongside later additions Scherrie Payne and Susaye Greene. The group officially disbanded due to the absence of a contract offer renewal from Motown Records and any other external offers. Although later recordings failed to achieve significant chart positions, the group's performances consistently attracted substantial crowds.

The B-side "This Is Why I Believe in You" is an uptempo number.

The Supremes' struggle to regain their status as a singles act is a compelling paradox of their story as they closed their final active year reaching number one on the British album chart with '20 Greatest Hits' part of an EMI Records catalogue repackage compilation series - in the case of the Supremes release it was released in conjunction with Motown Records compiling 20 of their Sixties recordings - the album also reached number one on the Blues and Soul Magazine British album chart and likewise on the (Black) Echoes British soul albums chart.

Footnote: Mary Wilson's steadfast commitment to preserving the Supremes' legacy and impact is a testament to her fortitude. Nonetheless, the Supremes' appellation was upheld by her. Following a moment of deliberation, she recognised the lasting value of the Supremes' brand and subsequently decided against pursuing an independent recording career. Through Cindy

Birdsong's rejoining and the subsequent recruitment of Scherrie Payne, the group attained a complete complement of a vocal trio. Wilson increased her lead vocal contributions, further developing those skills through vocal coaching.

Supremes Medley (Parts 1 &2)
(Tamla Motown TMG 1180) - UK Release Date : Apr 1980

This single's release, unfortunately ill-timed, preceded the surge in popularity of medley/megamix-themed singles that characterised the years 1981-1982, a trend largely driven by the Starsound releases.

This seamless megamix originated from the US (conflicting reports by whom constructed and commisioned it), regardless this medleymix consisted of a gimmick free sequence of the following tracks - Stop! In The Name Of Love/ Back In My Arms Again/Come See About Me/Love Is Like An Itching In My Heart/Where Did Our Love Go/Baby Love.

This medley saw release in a 7-inch vinyl format. Nonetheless, it proves more elusive than its 12-inch counterpart.

The song's success is evidenced by its inclusion in Blues and Soul magazine's British soul music chart, where it reached the top 25 and maintained its presence there for 14 weeks.

The 12-inch vinyl copies were backed by the full-length version of the Diana Ross solo disco track "Love Hangover".

The Composer b/w Take Me Where You Go

(Tamla Motown TMG 999)- UK Release Date: Apr 1985

The Motown Classics series features this compilation of twenty singles (TMG 989–TMG 999 and TMG 1380–TMG 1388), released in April 1985.

To clarify, it is understood that "The Composer" surfaced on an official UK-released Tamla Motown 45 in any capacity for the first time under this series.

"The Composer" had its official release as a 45 RPM single on German and Dutch Tamla Motown labels in 1969, also featuring on the group's 1969-released LP, 'Let the Sunshine In'. The B-side, "Take Me Where You Go," was included on the 1979 compilation album, 'From the Vaults,' which featured unreleased recordings.

Featured on their album 'Let the Sunshine In,' this song, a composition and production by Smokey Robinson, achieved a ranking within the top thirty on the American Billboard Hot 100 during the spring of 1969. Mirroring the standard practice for a number of Diana Ross-era Supremes singles of 1968-1969, background vocals were supplied by Motown session vocalists, The Andantes, instead of Mary Wilson and Cindy Birdsong. Among Supremes recordings, "The Composer" is unusual for its absence from televised performances.

No known British chart action on the back of this first time release on the single format.

Hit And Miss (Mixes)

(Motorcity Records 12 MOTC 88) - UK Release : 1991
AKA Jean, Scherrie & Lynda (Former Ladies) of the Supremes

In 1989, the British R&B producer and DJ Ian Levine established a British record label focused on recordings from artists who had previously worked with Motown, in an attempt to recreate the magic that Motown itself had pioneered almost three decades earlier.

An incarnation of The Supremes featuring no original members but members who had passed through the ranks during the '70s - in this case the members on this particular recording were Jean Terrell, Scherrie Payne & Lynda Laurence.

Prior to the recording and the release of this particular single, Ian Levine's contributions were essential to the success of various multi-artist package tours, comparable in style and structure to the original 1960s Motortown Revue. A month-long concert tour during the tail end of 1990. The performers on this tour belonged firmly to the 'Motown vintage' including Syreeta, Marv Johnson, Kim Weston, The Elgins and Carolyn Crawford culminating in a headline performance by (as billed as) Jean, Scherrie, and Lynda of The Supremes. A video recording of the tour's final night was later commercially released as a two-part home video set, 'Legends of Motorcity, USA'.

Co-wriiten by Lynda Laurence with Ian Levine, "Hit And Miss" a Hi-NRG/soul track was only available as a 12'-inch vinyl single , unfortunately no known chart action, considering the fact in a twisted levels of irony that in both Britain and in America that the Motown brand was getting renewed success in that era with a new generation of artists obtaining success signed to the label (Shanice, Boyz II Men) as well as the established and associated (Lionel Richie, Michael Jackson) and those from the classic era returning back into the charts (Diana Ross, Smokey Robinson, Temptations) but yet again no such returns for The Supremes in whatever incarnation it seems.

Back By Popular Demand (DJ Edit & Original Versions)

(Beatin Rhythm BRS 1001) - UK Release Date : 2011

Jean, Scherrie & Lynda, formerly of The Supremes with The Originals. A recording project, under the supervision of British R&B producer and DJ Ian Levine, featured three latter former members of the Supremes and members of their Motown contemporaries, The Originals.

April 1990 saw the sessions held at Entourage Studios, Hollywood. The synergistic union of two leading groups from the golden age of soul music. Subsequently, Jean Terrell's involvement with the group concluded after this recording. The record became a quintessential example of Northern Soul music and was taken from the previously unreleased 1991 album 'Bouncing Back'.

Following its initial release on Levine's Motorcity label, the song was subsequently re-released by Beatin' Rhythm Records approximately twenty years later.

This limited edition reissue vinyl record presents performances by The Supremes and The Originals, including "Back By Popular Demand" and "I'm Gonna Make You Love Me," showcasing Mod and Northern Soul styles. Its inclusion in any music enthusiast's collection is highly recommended.

Your Heart Belongs To Me b/w Interview with Brian Matthew

(Outta Sight RSV 053)- UK Release Date: 2014

"Your Heart Belongs To Me," the first Supremes track written and produced by Smokey Robinson, their former neighbour in the Brewster-Douglass housing project, marked a significant milestone in their career.

Released originally in 1962 by Motown as a single. This song portrays a woman whose paramour is a member of the armed forces; its narrative features her reminding him of their love should loneliness ever arise.

This single represented the last recording from The Supremes in their quartet configuration. Subsequent to this recording, Barbara Martin's departure to raise a family reduced the group to their trio familiarity of Diana Ross, Florence Ballard, and Mary Wilson. Martin's omission from the cover image is a result of her impending departure and her pregnancy, which was apparent during the photoshoot.

The song was a humbling chart entry on the American Hot 100.

Incidentally, the inclusion of all four Supremes on a single record was not achieved again until "I'm Gonna Let My Heart Do the Walking" was released in 1976.

The R&B specialty label, Outta Sight, issued an initial British release of "Your Heart Belongs to Me," which included a brief on-air radio interview from the original BBC radio series Top Gear. Brian Matthew hosted the interview, which was produced by Bernie Andrews. The Supremes presented themselves and subsequently elaborated upon matters related to the Apollo.

Top Supremes Hits On The UK Singles Chart

Statistics based on UK chart position performance peak - if a particular single shares an identikit peak, weeks on chart is taken into account with the one spending the most weeks being seen as the bigger hit.

1. Baby Love

2. Where Did Our Love Go

3. Stoned Love

4. I'm Gonna Make You Love Me (with The Temptations)

5. You Can't Hurry Love

6. Reflections

7. Nathan Jones

8. Up The Ladder To The Roof

9. The Happening

10. Stop! In The Name Of Love

11. You Keep Me Hanging On

12. Floy Joy

13. Automatically Sunshine

14. River Deep Mountain High (with The Four Tops)

15. Someday We'll Be Together

16. In And Out Of Love

17. I'm Living In Shame

18. Love Child

19. Love Is Here And Now You're Gone

20. I Second That Emotion (with The Temptations)

The others & the rest

A summary selection of known EP , promo releases and re-issues

The Supremes' Hits
Tamla Motown, UK, TME 2008, EP - UK Release Date: Apr 1965

A1: Where Did Our Love Go
A2: Baby Love
B1: Come See About Me
B2: When The Lovelight Starts Shining Thru' His Eyes
A four song EP comprising of their first four British releases

Shake
Tamla Motown, UK, TME 2011, EP - UK Release Date: Feb 1966

A1: Shake
A2: Chain Gang
B1: Havin' A Party
B2: Good News
A British-only EP adapted from the Sam Cooke-themed tribute album "We Remember Sam Cooke" , the Supremes' fifth studio album, which was released in 1965.

Anthology
Tamla Motown, UK, PSR 365, Promo Only 7" UK Release: 1974

A1: Baby Love
A2: You Can't Hurry Love
B1: The Happening
B2: Love Child
EP released as decade celebration of The Supremes as a chart act

Tamla Motown, UK, TMG 1044, 7" UK Release Date : Sep 1976

A: Baby Love
B: Stop! In The Name Of Love

Tamla Motown, UK, TMG 1046, 7"UK Release Date: Sep 1976

A: Stoned Love
B: Nathan Jones
Both above singles part of the 'Motown Singles Collection' series

Motown, UK, TMG 1080, 7"UK Release Date: Aug 1977

A: Someday We'll Be Together
B: You Keep Me Hangin' On

Tamla Motown, UK, TMG 956, 7" UK Release Date: Sep 1980

A: You Can't Hurry Love
B: The Happening

113

Tamla Motown, UK, TMG 964, 7"UK Release Date: Sep 1980,

A: Up The Ladder To The Roof
B: Automatically Sunshine

Tamla Motown, UK, TMG 971, 7" UK Release Date : Sep 1980

A: River Deep, Mountain High
B: You Gotta Have Love In Your Heart

Tamla Motown, UK, TMG 974, 7" UK Release Date: Sep 1980

A: Floy Joy
B: Bad Weather

Tamla Motown, UK, TMG 981, 7"UK Release Date: Feb 1983

A: Back In My Arms Again
B: Love Is Here And Now You're Gone

Tamla Motown, UK, TMG 991, 7"UK Release Date: Apr 1985

A: I'm Gonna Make You Love Me
B: I Second That Emotion

Tamla Motown, UK, TMG 992, 7"UK Release Date: Apr 1985

A: You Keep Me Hangin' On
B: Come See About Me

By this time in the UK and indeed other parts of the world , distribution had switched from EMI to the Bertlesmann RCA/Ariola set up and the above two singles represented a part of the 'The Motown Classics' re-issue series of classic mainly 60s era recordings from the rich back catalogues of the Motown roster

Tamla Motown, UK, ZB 40709, 7"UK Release Date: Apr 1986

A: You Keep Me Hangin' On
B: Come See About Me

Tamla Motown, UK, ZB 41931, 7" Release: 1988

A: Up The Ladder To The Roof
B: Floy Joy

Tamla Motown, UK, ZB 41925, 7" UK Release Date: Mar 1988

A: Someday We'll Be Together
B: My World Is Empty Without You

Motown, UK, ZB 41963, 7" UK Release Date: Feb 1989

A: Stop! In The Name Of Love
B: Automatically Sunshine

Motorcity MOTC 13, 7" and 12" UK Release:1989 * as FLOS

A: Crazy Bout The Guy
B:Crazy Bout The Guy (Instrumental)

The following releases were issued pursuant to a long-term distribution agreement deal between Motown Records and Universal Music Group, the latter having actually acquired the Motown Records catalogue in 1991and til this day distributes the artists and the label's catalogue re-issue programmes between their frontline labels like Polydor, Island and rather ironically the EMI-Capitol set up.

Tamla Motown, UK, 982 155 1, 7" UK Release Date: Aug 2004

A: Baby Love
B: Where Did Our Love Go

Tamla Motown, UK, 533 829-9, Shaped Disc, UK Release Date: Apr 2012

A: Baby Love
B: Stop In The Name Of Love (Alternate Take)

Stateside, UK, 535 414-7, 7"UK Release Date: Dec 2014

A: Come See About Me
B: When The Lovelight Starts Shining Thru' His Eyes

Tamla Motown, UK, 537 211-7, EP , UK Release Date: Jan 2017

A1: Where Did Our Love Go
A2: Baby Love
B1: Come See About Me
B2: When The Lovelight Starts Shining Through His Eyes

Dynamite Cuts , UK BYNAM 7124, "12, UK Release :2024 *As The Supremes V Magic Disco Machine*

A: Bend A Little (Supremes)
B:Bend A Little (Magic Disco Machine)

Two iterations of this dance track exist for the first time on double sided vinyl. "Bend a Little" by The Supremes whilst the instrumental funk outfit Magic Disco Machine offers the instrumental version and it surfaced on club classic specialists Dynamite Cuts.

Also by the author…

The rundown to the Christmas number one single is always an event, with pundits, producers and the artists themselves waiting to see what the British music buying public have chosen to dominate the festive season's chart rundown. From the traditional balladry of Al Martino's 'Here In My Heart' way back in 1952 to the fresh contemporary sounds of Clean Bandit in 2016, this is the ultimate guide to those number one singles.

The stories of those songs reflect eras of change, sometimes upbeat and ligh-hearted, at other times grim and difficult.

Through wide-ranging research and a feel for historical context, the author weaves a comprehensive tapestry of the people and sounds that dominated our lives during holiday seasons past.

Available at  **and:**

victorpublishing.co.uk/shop

Got a book in you?

This book is published by Victor Publishing. Victor Publishing specialises in getting new and independent writers' work published worldwide in both paperback and Kindle format. We also look to re-publish titles that were previously published but have now gone out of circulation or off-sale. If you have a manuscript for a book (or have previously published a now off-sale title) of any genre (fiction, non-fiction, autobiographical, biographical or even reference or photographic/illustrative) and would like more information on how you can get your work published and on sale in print and digitally,
please visit us at:
www.victorpublishing.co.uk
or get in touch at: enquiries@victorpublishing.co.uk

Printed in Dunstable, United Kingdom

66573880R00067